CAMMI
GRANATO

CAMMI GRANATO

Hockey Pioneer

Thom Loverro

LERNER
SPORTS
AN IMPRINT OF LERNER PUBLISHING GROUP

This book is available in two editions:
Library binding by LernerSports
Soft cover by First Avenue Editions
Imprints of Lerner Publishing Group
241 First Avenue North
Minneapolis, Minnesota 55401 U.S.A.

Website address: www.lernerbooks.com

Library of Congress Cataloging-in-Publication Data

Loverro, Thom.
    Cammi Granato, hockey pioneer / by Thom Loverro.
      p. cm.
    Includes bibliographical references (p.) and index.
    Summary: A biography of the American who was captain of the first Olympic gold medal-winning women's hockey team.
    ISBN 0−8225−3682−X (lib. bdg. : alk. paper)
    ISBN 0−8225−9862−0 (pbk. : alk. paper)
    1. Granato, Cammi, 1971—Juvenile literature. 2. Hockey players—United States—Biography—Juvenile literature. 3. Women hockey players—United States—Biography—Juvenile literature.
[1. Granato, Cammi, 1971− 2. Hockey players. 3. Women—Biography] I. Title.
GV848.5.G69 A3 2000
796.962'092—dc21
                                                    00−008851

Manufactured in the United States of America
1 2 3 4 5 6 − JR − 05 04 03 02 01 00

Contents

1 Gold Medal Moment   7

2 Miracle on Ice   15

3 College and the
World Beyond   25

4 Heading for the Olympics   35

5 Being the First   45

Glossary   59

Sources   62

Index   63

Gold Medal Moment

Riding to the Olympic ice arena, Cammi Granato could hardly believe where she was and what she was about to do. Soon she and her U. S. teammates would be playing a game that would decide who would win the first Olympic gold medal for women's ice hockey.

Cammi, a captain and **forward** on the U. S. women's hockey team, was one of the stars at the 1998 Olympic Winter Games in Nagano, Japan. As she thought about the upcoming showdown against her team's longtime rival, Canada, Cammi felt confident in her skills and her preparation. This was the moment she had been dreaming of her whole life.

During the bus ride to Big Hat, the arena where the game would be held, Cammi's team watched parts of the film *When We Were Kings*. The award-winning movie is about boxing champion Muhammad Ali and his historic fight with George Foreman in Africa. The U. S. coaches also showed some highlights of the women's team. "That tape really pumped us up," forward Lisa Brown-Miller later said. "I had tears in my eyes, and I could see us succeeding."

Inspired and energized, the players raced to their locker room when they arrived at the arena. Cammi, as always, touched her lucky stuffed frog in her locker. There, she found a note from her sister, Christine, that read, "Go for the gold."

The excited crowd of 10,000 cheered as the big game began. Play in the first period was slow., and neither team scored. American goaltender Sarah Tueting stopped 15 Canadian shots in the first period alone. The game heated up in the second period. American forward Gretchen Ulion took the puck at the **left face-off circle.** She skated a few steps and then whipped the puck over the shoulder of Canadian goalie Manon Rheaume to score. The U. S. team had a 1—0 lead after two periods. Could the Americans hold on for another period?

Cammi cheers as her team gets the puck past the Canadian goaltender in the Olympic championship.

U. S. forward Shelley Looney deflected a shot by teammate Sandra Whyte just past Rheaume's leg to give the Americans a 2–0 lead with less than 10 minutes left in the game. "It was the longest 10 minutes of my life," said Cammi later. "I just wanted it to be over."

About six minutes after Looney's goal, the Canadians answered. With the Canadian team on the **power play,** forward Danielle Goyette got a pass from behind the American net. She slipped the puck past Tueting to cut the U. S. lead to 2−1. The Americans could feel the pressure, but they stayed focused. "After they scored, we all reminded ourselves what we had dedicated our lives to and settled down and played like we knew we could," said defender Angela Ruggiero.

Cammi and her team knew that they could win if they kept playing strong defense. "We wanted to keep doing what we had been doing," said Cammi. "The whole game I was thinking of this dream of winning a gold medal."

With just 54 seconds left in the game, the Canadians pulled Rheaume out of the goal to add another skater on the ice. The strategy didn't work. Instead, the Americans got control of the puck, and Whyte slapped it into the empty net with just eight seconds left. Cammi watched as the seconds ticked off the clock . . . three . . . two . . . one. . . .

The buzzer sounded, and the crowd in the arena went wild. The U. S. women's team exploded in cheers. Sticks and gloves flew in the air as Cammi and her teammates swarmed Tueting at the goal. Cammi looked to the stands to share the moment with her family. "I could see the look in their eyes," Cammi said. "You could see how proud they were."

The U. S. players celebrate their gold medal!

The fans in the Big Hat were caught up in the excitement and ready to celebrate, but they had to wait a bit. While the ice was being prepared for the medal ceremony, the American players disappeared into their locker room. They had planned to gather there if they won. "We went back and had a toast to our team," Cammi said. "I sat back in my stall and kind of lost it. It really hit me at that point. I had to gather myself so I could get back on the ice for the medals and the anthem."

Cammi and her teammates walked onto the ice and held hands while waiting for their gold medals. Fans stood and roared as Cammi's medal was placed around her neck. "Karen [Bye] leaned over to me and said, 'This is the first gold medal ever,' and the weight of that struck me so much, I nearly lost my composure again," Cammi said. "It was an amazing feeling. All of your hard work has paid off at that moment. It's something that you dreamed about, something that you visualized. And when it actually happens, it's very emotional."

Cammi's dream had begun some 18 years before. That's when she found a hero as she watched the 1980 U. S. men's Olympic hockey team defeat the mighty Soviet squad.

Cammi and Karen Bye show off their gold medals.

Miracle on Ice

On February 2, 1980, Cammi and her brothers—Tony, Donny, Joey, and Robby—sat around the television set in their Downer's Grove, Illinois, home with their parents, Don and Natalie, and their sister, Christina. As they watched, the U. S. men's hockey team, a team of untested and inexperienced players, defeated the powerful Soviet team. The Olympic upset came to be known as the "Miracle on Ice."

The thrilling victory impressed the Granato children. U. S. men's hockey team members Ken Morrow, Jim Craig, and Mike Eruzione became their heroes. The Granato kids did their best to imitate them, using tape to mark out a rink in the basement.

Cammi started being a Blackhawks fan when she was 15 months old and got this jersey.

They taped up a tissue ball to use for a puck. Cammi pretended to be forward Mike Eruzione, who scored the game-winning goal against the Russians that broke the 3—3 tie. (The United States won the 1980 gold medal by beating Finland in the next game.)

When they weren't playing hockey in the basement, the Granato kids played on a frozen pond near their house or on their own flooded yard. The whole family loved hockey so much that the Granatos even took vacations at hockey camps. When the Granato children did book reports for school, they wrote about hockey books.

Catherine Michelle Granato was born on March 25, 1971, the fifth of six children. Her parents had no idea that she would become a hockey superstar. Cammi's brothers were already playing sports, including hockey, but most girls didn't play hockey in the 1970s. If girls wanted to skate, they took figure skating lessons. So when Cammi was five, her mother signed her up for figure skating. But Cammi wanted to play hockey like her brothers. "Finally we just stopped fighting it," Cammi's father, Don, said. After that, Cammi's parents did their best to help her play the game.

Robby and Cammi play some sidewalk hockey.

Cammi began playing on a hockey team with one of her brothers and a cousin. She had to endure a lot of teasing from other players, coaches, and parents. "She had to change in the girls' bathroom while her teammates dressed together in locker rooms," Cammi's mother, Natalie, said. "There would be some comments and snickers from other mothers and other little girls who were figure skaters."

Cammi is in the front row and the third player from right in this photograph of her AA peewee team.

Although Cammi didn't know it at the time, there were others like her across the country. Some of them would grow up to be her teammates.

But before the 1980s, there weren't many opportunities for girls in organized hockey. In 1972, Congress passed a law called **Title IX.** The law said that schools had to offer girls the same opportunities in sports as boys had if the schools received federal money. Not many schools obeyed the law at first. As more and more schools began adding sports for girls, more girls began playing sports, and they began playing sports that had once been reserved for boys. High schools and colleges began sponsoring teams, leagues, and championships in many different sports.

When she was growing up, Cammi played in boys' leagues because there were no girls' hockey leagues. According to her mother, "As Cammi got older and the boys she played against got bigger and stronger, it was tough because she was singled out and they tried to hurt her physically. She had quite a few serious injuries, like concussions, sprained shoulders, different things like that." Sometimes Cammi traded jerseys with a teammate so it would be harder for other players to target her.

Although Cammi's parents knew she loved to play hockey, they were often worried about her. One time, Cammi got slammed and knocked down. She was hurt so badly that she didn't want to get up, but she did. "My dad was behind the glass about five feet away," Cammi said. "I wanted to stay down so much. After the game, my dad asked if it hurt and I said no. I was afraid he would make me quit."

Cammi soon learned the rules she would have to live by if she wanted to keep playing the game she loved. She learned not to cry or run to her parents when her brothers smacked her against the boards. Her brothers warned her that if she did, they would not play with her anymore. "She would get bumped or bruised, or get a stick in the face, and she would be right back in there," Cammi's brother Tony recalled. "It took me until I was 16 or 17 before I realized that she was doing something most other little sisters aren't doing."

Cammi also learned that she would have to do whatever it took to play competitive hockey. Sometimes that meant tucking her hair inside of her helmet and pretending she was a boy. One coach listed her as "Carl" on his roster when her team played in a tournament that did not allow girls to play.

When she was 13, Cammi won a trophy at an All Star tournament.

"I couldn't understand why, just because I was a girl, hockey wasn't an acceptable activity for me in society," Cammi said. "I wanted to play the game because I loved the game."

As Cammi grew older, playing hockey became more difficult for her. By the time she turned 15, she simply couldn't take the beating from the bigger and stronger boys she competed against. So Cammi looked for other ways to fulfill her athletic goals. She played soccer and basketball throughout high school on girls' teams and played team handball at two U. S. Olympic Festivals. The Olympic Festival is a sports event that is sponsored by amateur sports organizations in the United States to show off talented youngsters in Olympic sports.

Still, Cammi dreamed of hockey. She dreamed of playing for an Olympic gold medal. She dreamed of playing in the National Hockey League (NHL). "She told me she wanted to play for the [Chicago] Blackhawks," her mother said. "I probably laughed, not knowing how much she cared. I said, 'Honey, it's not going to work because girls don't play in the NHL.' It probably broke her heart."

Cammi, No. 10, with her high school basketball team

Cammi, No. 21, with her high school soccer team

Cammi's brother Tony made the 1988 U. S. men's Olympic hockey team that competed at the Games in Calgary, Alberta. Seeing her brother play in the Olympics made Cammi, then nearly 17, want to reach her goal even more. "The 1980 team really did something to me," said Cammi, "but when I got a chance to see my brother up close at the 1988 Games and I saw what a wonderful experience it was, I wanted to be part of it."

Cammi, top right, with Providence College teammates

College and the World Beyond

Although Cammi's goal seemed almost impossible, women's hockey was slowly growing. In 1987, the Ontario Women's Hockey Association had hosted the first women's World Invitational Tournament. The tournament featured women's hockey teams from Canada, the United States, Sweden, Switzerland, Holland, and Japan. Supporters and organizers of women's hockey wanted the International Ice Hockey Federation (IIHF) to sponsor a Women's World Championship like the men's tournament it already ran.

Even though she hadn't had a high school hockey team to play on, after Cammi graduated from high school in 1989, she received a **scholarship** offer from Providence College. Providence was a hotbed of women's hockey. In 1984, Providence College had won the very first Eastern College Athletic Conference (ECAC) Women's Championship. Women's hockey teams from colleges in the eastern part of the United States competed in the ECAC tournament, making it the closest thing to a national championship at the time.

Providence, which is in Rhode Island, did not often offer scholarships to girls from Illinois. Most of its students came from New England, where there were more hockey opportunities for young women. An assistant coach at Providence had once seen Cammi play in an amateur tournament. Cammi's skills stood out, and the Providence coaches didn't hesitate to ask her to join their team.

Cammi had other scholarship offers, too, but those were from colleges that wanted her to play soccer or basketball. Cammi also thought of sticking with team handball and trying to make the Olympic team in that sport. But since hockey was her passion, she decided to go to Providence.

Cammi in action for Providence College

"I felt like I had betrayed hockey by not playing [in high school], and getting a scholarship to play hockey was a dream come true," Cammi said.

Cammi became Providence's star player. Three times she was chosen as the ECAC Women's Hockey Player of the Year. She scored 139 goals in her four seasons at Providence and led the Lady Friars to two ECAC championships.

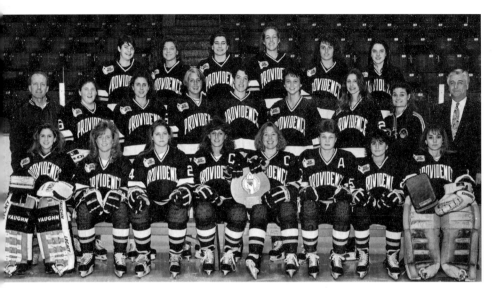

*Cammi, front row, fourth from left, and the rest of the
1992-93 ECAC champions*

And she didn't just play for Providence. The most
talented athletes from all over the United States are
invited each year to try out for the national team,
which represents the United States in tournaments
all over the world. Cammi played for the U. S. national team all four years she was in college.

In 1990, the IIHF sponsored its first world championship for women. The tournament took place in
Ottawa, Ontario. Led by Cammi, the U. S. team
reached the championship, where the Americans
would face the powerful Canadian squad. In the final

game, the Americans took an early 2—0 lead. But Canada came back to score a 5—2 victory.

It wasn't as close the next time the two teams met. In the 1992 international championships in Tampere, Finland, Canada destroyed the United States 8—0 in the final game. Cammi went home with yet another silver medal. Finland finished third.

Cammi and Providence teammates celebrate their title.

Cammi led all scorers at the tournament with eight goals and two **assists** in five games. She was named the tournament's best forward and was selected for the all-tournament team. Just two Americans were picked for the 1992 all-tournament team—Cammi and defender Ellen Weinberg.

After graduating from Providence in 1993, Cammi did all she could to keep following her dream—a dream that had moved closer to reality. Just before Cammi graduated from Providence College, the International Olympic Committee approved women's hockey as a medal sport for the 1998 Olympic Games. Cammi's dream could come true if she and her teammates could make it happen.

Cammi and her teammates finally defeated Canada in 1993. Women's ice hockey was included in the U. S. Olympic Festival for the first time. The U. S. team defeated Canada in a two-game series for the gold medal at the Festival.

After college, Cammi coached a youth hockey team for boys in Wisconsin before she decided to enroll in graduate school at Concordia University in Montreal, Quebec.

Many American women hockey players go to school in Canada after they have finished college.

Cammi, center, helps the U. S. team take home the silver from the world championships in 1992.

The organization that runs college athletics in the United States is called the National Collegiate Athletic Association (NCAA). According to NCAA rules, an athlete can only play sports in American colleges for four years.

Cammi suits up for Concordia.

But, if an athlete goes to a college outside of the United States, she can continue to play sports for another four years. Playing hockey in graduate school for four years gave Cammi a chance to improve against the top Canadian players.

"When I got out of college, I had a lot of decisions to make," Cammi said. "A lot of my friends were getting real jobs. I sat down with my parents and said financially this isn't the best situation for me, but this is something I want to do. Once I got their support, it was easy to make the decision, and it was the best decision I could have made. I had to make some sacrifices if I wanted to keep playing hockey. But deep inside I knew I had so much more hockey left to play."

Cammi has played for the U. S. national team every year since the team was started.

Heading for the Olympics

At the 1994 Women's World Championships, it was the same old story. Cammi led the U. S. team in scoring with five goals and seven assists in five games. But once again, the U. S. team came up short. Canada won the championship with a 6–3 victory over the United States, and Finland took the bronze. The Canadians just dominated international women's hockey.

Canada again defeated the United States in the championship of the 1995 IIHF Pacific Rim tournament, this time in a heartbreaking overtime. Once again, Cammi was the tournament-leading scorer, scoring four goals and seven assists. She tied team-mates Karen Bye and Stephanie Boyd with 11 **points** in five games.

Cammi showed her talent again at the 1996 IIHF Pacific Rim Championships. She was the tournament's leading scorer with six goals and three assists in five games. She was also named the tournament's outstanding forward. But, it all added up to another silver medal as Canada beat the United States 4−1 in the championship.

By 1996, Cammi was the best-known player in women's hockey. The New York Islanders invited her to play at their **training camp.** She would have been the first female non-goaltender to attend a National Hockey League training camp. The offer—a chance to compete, even if it was just in a training camp, with NHL players—tempted Cammi. She thought it was probably as close as she would get to her dream of playing for the Chicago Blackhawks. She talked it over with her brother Tony, who was playing in the NHL for the San Jose Sharks. Then Cammi said "No." She didn't want her NHL tryout to be thought of as a joke. And, with the Olympic Games just two years off, Cammi didn't want to risk getting injured.

*Cammi's oldest brother, Tony, plays right wing for the
San Jose Sharks in the National Hockey League.*

On August 27, 1996, after six days and 24 games among 54 players, USA Hockey officials and coaches chose 25 players to be on the first American women's Olympic hockey team. Selecting the athletes was difficult but it wasn't hard for the coaches to decide that Cammi belonged on the team. With her international experience as a leader, Cammi was named a team captain.

"Making it this far puts me where I have always wanted to be," said Cammi. "To hear my name called was such a relief, and I am very happy to be on this team with so many of my really good friends." Three of the players chosen—Cammi, Lisa Brown-Miller, and Kelly O'Leary—had been on every national team since 1990, when the team started.

The national team played **exhibition games** to tune up for the Nagano Olympics. The Olympians played during the National Hockey League's All-Star Game weekend. They lost a hard-fought 2—1 game to the Canadian team before a crowd of 14,000.

After seeing all the fans at the women's hockey game on All-Star weekend, the president of the United States Olympic Committee, Bill Hybl, said, "The story of the Winter Games in Nagano will be women's hockey."

Cammi and her teammates polished their skills in exhibition games before the Olympics.

Cammi received a special treat at the NHL All-Star event. Mike Eruzione, the forward on the 1980 "Miracle on Ice" team whom she had tried to copy on her family's rink, practiced with the women's team and offered the players advice and inspiration.

Unlike the famous 1980 men's team, the U. S. women's rival would not be the former Soviet Union. Women's hockey in Russia was far behind the quality of play in other countries. In a March 1997 exhibition game at Lake Placid—where the "Miracle on Ice" game took place—the American women easily defeated the Russian team 7—0. The U. S. team went on to play an exhibition series against Sweden and Finland. The Americans won all six games.

The pre-Olympic games showed the intense rivalry that had built up between the United States and Canada. The two teams played 13 games against each other before the Olympics. All the games drew large crowds. A packed arena in Salt Lake City, Utah, cheered when Cammi scored in a shootout to defeat the Canadians, 5—4. At a game in San Jose, California, a crowd of 8,000 watched the United States tie Canada with just seven seconds left and then go on to win 4—3 in overtime. "We play before crowds of 10,000 or more," said Cammi. "It used to be we played in buildings with our moms and dads and not much else."

Then, in December 1997, the U. S. team shut out the Canadian team, 3—0, in the finals of the Three Nations Cup, which features the United States, Canada, and Finland. It was a bruising game even though **body-checking** is prohibited in the women's game. The victory gave the U. S. team confidence. "We mentally know we can beat this team," Cammi said after the game. "It's not as if there is a gap anymore."

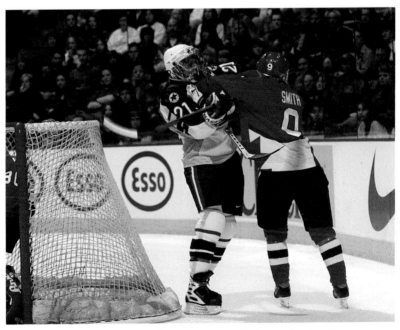

The rivalry between the U. S. and Canada is fierce.

As the best-known woman playing hockey in America, Cammi felt she should promote hockey for girls and women. She wouldn't let that responsibility get in the way of her ultimate goal, however. "If I'm going to be a spokeswoman, I can accept that role," Cammi said. "I enjoy talking about the sport, and I have experience with that. But I also don't want to get caught up in any hoopla. I want to be focused on beating the Canadians."

For Cammi and her teammates, winning the Olympic gold medal meant beating the Canadians. In the 13 games between the two teams in the pre-Olympic tour, the Canadians edged the Americans seven games to six. The Americans won three of their last four games before the Canadians won the series with a 4—2 victory just before leaving for Japan. The two teams were so close that they were tied in total points scored for the 13 games. Each team had scored 37 points.

On the pre-Olympic tour, Cammi was one of the U. S. team's top scorers with 31 points—14 goals and 17 assists—in 29 games. In 11 of the 13 games against Canada, Cammi scored three goals and had three assists. Going into the Nagano Olympics, Cammi was the national team's all-time leading scorer with 37 goals and 27 assists in 30 games.

Women's hockey had grown significantly since Cammi had begun playing. In 1990, about 6,000 female players were registered to play the game on some level with USA Hockey. By 1997, there were nearly 24,000 players. Cammi and her teammates wanted to win the gold medal, but they also wanted to promote women's hockey through their play at the Olympics.

"There are so many great stories about sacrifices and everything that goes into being an Olympian, and that's what we're about, too," Cammi said. "Hopefully, people will get that into their minds and take a positive attitude about women's hockey, and get rid of the negative stereotypes, the people who say, 'You don't belong out there. What are you trying to do? It's a man's game.'"

The U. S. opened its gold-medal drive against China.

Being the First

As the 1998 Winter Olympics began in Nagano, Cammi let the world know that nothing short of a gold medal would satisfy the American women's team. "We are going with our sights set on the gold," she told reporters. "That is a very realistic goal for our team. We are not looking for anything else."

Even though his team had a game that afternoon, U. S. coach Ben Smith encouraged his players to take part in the opening ceremonies. Cammi and her teammates walked behind the American flag in the procession into the stadium. "It struck me when we got on the field," Cammi said. "It was like, 'I can't believe this is me doing this.' "

Cammi said she could sense that her teammates were ready for what was ahead of them when they played an exhibition game against the Japanese team and won easily, 10–0. But the Olympic competition didn't officially begin until the U. S. women took the ice against China in the opening game. Cammi scored the first goal by an American woman in the Olympics when she snapped in a **rebound** at 7:39 of the first period in a 5–0 victory. "It was a great feeling," Cammi said. "It was something I was thinking about for a long time. When I hit it in, it was sort of a relief." With 3:40 remaining in the game, she ended the scoring with her second goal, which came off a rebound from forward Katie King.

Cammi's teammates looked up to her, and they were happy that she was the first player to score a goal. "Cammi's a great player," said defender Tara Mounsey, who also scored two goals during the game. "There ought to be a lot of young girls looking up to number 21 [Cammi's number]. She should be a role model for a lot of little kids."

Next the U. S. team faced Sweden. The Americans had beaten the Swedish team many times before, including three times in their pre-Olympic tour. The Swedish team proved to be as beatable in Nagano.

Cammi slices through two Swedish defenders.

The U. S. team won 7−1. During the game, six different Americans scored goals. "We don't have to rely
on one player, one line, or one unit," the U. S. coach
said. "We have a team with good balance and depth."

Finland was a much stiffer test for the United
States. The Americans opened the scoring on a
nifty rebound goal by forward Vicki Movessian.

Cammi had her hands full against the Finns.

Finland tied the game with a power-play goal with less than two minutes left in the first period. Scoring in the second mirrored the first, with the Americans taking a 2–1 lead and Finland tying the score.

But within a minute, the United States went back ahead on a goal by Mounsey. The Americans went on to win 4−2. The victory over Finland was important for the U. S. team. The only team standing in the Americans' way to the gold-medal game was Japan.

Cammi shoots at the Japanese goaltender.

The U.S. team repeated its earlier success against the Japanese with a 10—0 victory.

Even though the Americans had qualified for the gold-medal game, they still had one more game to play in the **round-robin tournament**. The game was against Canada, which also qualified for the gold-medal game with a 4—2 victory over Finland.

The game between the Americans and the Canadians was more than competitive. It was the most intense, hard-fought women's game ever. The fierce rivalry between the two teams showed on the ice through their rough play. The U. S. team had players in the **penalty box** for 22 penalty minutes. The Canadian team served 18 minutes.

Going into the third period, Canada led 4—1. But the Americans scored six goals in the last period to win 7—4. Cammi scored two goals and handed out one assist in the game. But her contribution was barely noticed. A bitter controversy grabbed all the attention. During the game, U. S. forward Sandra Whyte had gotten into an argument with Canadian forward Danielle Goyette. Canadian coach Shannon Miller said that she heard Whyte say something about Goyette's 77-year-old father, who had died just before the Olympics began. After the game, Cammi skated across the ice to speak to coach Miller. "Things were misunderstood," Cammi said. "It got blown out of proportion."

What was not blown out of proportion, however, was the intense rivalry between the two teams. After all those tough losses against the Canadians in international competition, the U. S. players realized their dream with the victory in the gold-medal game.

Cammi celebrates the first women's hockey gold medal!

The story of the American women winning the gold medal was the biggest news to come out of the Winter Olympics in Nagano. The U. S. players were front-page news all across the country.

General Mills put their picture on the cover of a Wheaties cereal box. When the team arrived back home, Cammi appeared on morning television shows, *The Late Show with David Letterman,* commercials for AT&T, and in many interviews.

The U. S. team had achieved its goal of creating more interest in women's hockey. "I hope this provides opportunities for girls that we didn't have when we were little," said Cammi.

In the midst of all the attention, some players and fans talked about someday starting a women's professional hockey league. The Buffalo Wings of Major League Roller Hockey drafted Cammi, but she turned down the offer.

Cammi was faced with decisions about her future. She had realized her dream. What was next for her? Cammi still loved hockey, but there weren't many opportunities for women to play the game. "I'd like to get some experience coaching on the collegiate level and then we'll see what is down the road. I still enjoy playing," said Cammi.

Cammi's success made her popular with sportscasters and sportswriters all over the country.

Then the Los Angeles Kings, an NHL team, hired Cammi to be a commentator for the team's radio broadcasts for the 1998-1999 season. Cammi was just the second woman to hold such a job in the league. The job challenged Cammi but gave her the time to play in national team tournaments.

Cammi played in several charity games for the Los Angeles Kings. In this game, one of her teammates was the legendary Wayne Gretzky, center.

"I would have been crazy not to take this job," she said. "But the number one thing to me was that they would give me the time to skate on their team. I wasn't ready to give that up." Cammi stayed sharp on the ice by working out with Kings players and coaches. She surprised some of them. "I was really surprised with her skill level, as I think all the coaches are," said Kings assistant coach Don Edwards. "She's a talented lady."

Cammi also continued her work in promoting and developing hockey opportunities for girls. "My brothers and I put on a hockey camp near Chicago, and we had 170 girls come," she said. "That's just phenomenal."

Cammi supports youth hockey programs for girls.

Cammi poses with her brothers and sister. Robby and Donny are in the front row. In the back row, from the left, are Joey, Christine, Cammi, and Tony.

Cammi has become a teacher and commentator for the game, but she remains a player. Following the 1998 Winter Games, USA Hockey decided to put together a national women's hockey team for six months of training and international competition each year leading up to the Olympic Games in 2002.

Cammi and 14 other members of the 1998 team will try out for a run at another gold medal. If they are successful, it will just be the icing on the cake for Cammi. "I feel blessed," Cammi said. "Other women didn't get to play in the Olympics or get that gold. I did."

Career Highlights

Providence College

Season	Games Played	Goals	Assists	Points
1989-90	21	24	22	46
1990-91	24	26	20	46
1991-92	25	48	32	80
1992-93	29	41	43	84
Totals	**99**	**139**	**117**	**256**

Concordia College

Season	Games Played	Goals	Assists	Points
1993-94	20	28	32	60
1994-95	35	45	35	80
1995-96	42	70	49	119
1996-97	28	36	35	71
Totals	**125**	**179**	**151**	**330**

Team USA

Season	Event	Games Played	Goals	Assists	Points
1990	World Championship	5	9	5	14
1992	World Championship	5	8	2	10
1994	World Championship	5	5	7	12
1995	Women's Championship	5	4	7	11
1996	Three Nations Cup	5	5	1	6
1996	Women's Championship	5	6	3	9
1997	World Championship	5	5	3	8
1997	Three Nations Cup	4	2	2	4
1997–98	Pre-Olympic Tour	29	14	17	31
1998	Olympics	6	4	4	8
1998	Three Nations Cup	4	0	2	2
1999	World Championship	5	3	5	8
1999–2000	Select Tour	20	17	25	42
Totals		**99**	**80**	**81**	**161**

Glossary

assist: A pass to a teammate that results in a goal.

body-checking: The act of using one's body to block or hit another player so that the other player loses control of the puck. Body-checking is legal in many youth leagues and in men's hockey, but it is not allowed in women's hockey.

exhibition game: A game that is played by regular rules and with game officials but does not count in any league standings or season record.

forward: One of three skaters whose primary responsibility is to score. The forward in the middle is called the *center.* The forward on the right is the *right winger,* and the forward on the left is the *left winger.* Together, the three forwards make up a *line.*

left face-off circle: The face-off circle that is to the left of the defending goaltender. There are five face-off circles on the ice. One is in the center of the rink. There are two face-off circles in each team's zone—one to the right of the goaltender and one to the goalie's left. In the photograph on page 60, Cammi is in the left face-off circle.

Cammi wins the face-off by getting the puck to her teammate. One player from each team tries to get control of the puck after the official drops it.

penalty box: The bench area a player sits in when she has broken a rule of the game.

points: Credits given to a player for scoring a goal or assisting on one. A player gets one point for a goal and one point for an assist.

power play: The offense used when one's team has more players on the ice because the other team has one or more players in the penalty box.

rebound: The bouncing of the puck back into play after a goaltender has made a save.

round-robin tournament: A tournament in which each team plays every other team in a pre-set order.

scholarship: Money a college or organization gives a student to pay for his or her education. Colleges often award scholarships to outstanding students, athletes, musicians, and leaders.

Title IX: A federal law that requires any school that receives money from the government to provide equal sports opportunities for girls and boys.

training camp: The time before a season begins that the players on a team spend getting in shape and practicing with each other.

Sources

Information for this book was obtained from the author's interviews with Cammi and other members of the 1998 U. S. Olympic hockey team and the following sources: Maureen Delany (*The Press Enterprise,* 5 February 1998); Bonnie DeSimone (*Chicago Tribune,* 3 February 1998); Michael Farber (*CNNSI.com,* 1997); Sharon Raboin (*USA Today,* 27 February 1998); *Scripps Howard News Service* (31 May 1997); Sport (April 1999); Mark Starr and Debra Rosenberg (*Newsweek,* 24 March 1997); USA Hockey; United States Olympic Committee media guide (1998).

Index

Boyd, Stephanie, 36
Brown-Miller, Lisa, 8, 38
Bye, Karen, 12, 13, 36

Concordia College, 30, 32—33

Eastern College Athletic
    Conference (ECAC), 26—27,
    28
Eruzione, Mike, 15, 16, 40

Goyette, Danielle, 10, 50—51
Granato, Christine (sister) 8, 56
Granato, Don (father), 15, 17,
    20
Granato, Donny (brother), 15,
    56
Granato, Joey (brother), 15, 56
Granato, Natalie (mother), 15,
    18, 19, 22
Granato, Robby (brother), 15,
    56
Granato, Tony (brother), 15, 20,
    23, 36, 37, 56

King, Katie, 46

Looney, Shelley, 9

Miller, Shannon, 50—51
Mounsey, Tara, 46
Movessian, Vicki, 47, 49

National Hockey League, 36,
    38, 40, 53
1980 Winter Olympic Games,
    12, 15—16, 40
1988 Winter Olympic Games,
    23
1998 Winter Olympic Games,
    7—13, 38, 44—52

O'Leary, Kelly, 38

Providence College, 24,
    26—27, 28, 29, 30

Rheaume, Manon, 8, 9, 10
Ruggiero, Angela, 10

Smith, Ben, 45, 47

Title IX, 19
Tueting, Sarah, 8, 10, 11

U. S. national team, 28—30, 34,
    35—36, 38—43, 57
Ulion, Gretchen, 8

Weinberg, Ellen, 30
Whyte, Sandra, 9, 10, 50—51

Write to Cammi:

You can send mail to Cammi at the address on the right. If you write a letter, don't get your hopes up too high. Cammi and other athletes get lots of letters every day, and they aren't always able to answer them all.

Cammi Granato
USA Hockey
1775 Bob Johnson Drive
Colorado Springs, CO
80906-4090

Acknowledgments

Photographs reproduced with permission of: © Bruce Bennett/Bruce Bennett Studios, 1, 6, 37, 41, 44, 47, 48, 51, 53, 54, 60; Sports Information Department, Providence College, 2, 27, 28; Reuters/Gary Hershorn/Archive Photos, 9, 49; © ALLSPORT USA/Al Bello, 11; Reuters/Mike Blake/Archive Photos, 13; Private collection of the Granato family, 14, 16, 17, 18, 21, 22, 23, 24, 29, 31, 32, 34, 55, 56; © Chris Trotman/DUOMO, 39.
Front cover photograph © Bruce Bennett/Bruce Bennett Studios.
Back cover photograph © Chris Trotman/DUOMO.

Artwork by Michael Tacheny.

About the Author

Thom Loverro is a sports columnist for *The Washington Times* newspaper in Washington, D. C. He has written two other books: *The Washington Redskins: The Authorized History* (Taylor Publishing) and *Home of the Game: The Story of Camden Yards* (Taylor Publishing). He is also on the adjunct faculty at American University where he teaches journalism. He lives in Columbia, Maryland, with his wife and two sons.